The Old Outer Hebrides

From Barra Head to the Butt of Lewis

With Kisimul Castle in the background, the steamer *Staffa* sits at Castlebay pier. Built in 1861 as the *Adela*, she was renamed when she came into the David MacBrayne fleet in 1887 and worked the mail run to the islands between 1888 and 1903.

First Published in the United Kingdom, 2011
Stenlake Publishing Limited
54-58 Mill Square, Catrine, KA5 6RD
01290 551122
www.stenlake.co.uk

ISBN 978 1 84033 569 9

A stall selling baubles, bangles and confectionery at a Uist fair.

Acknowledgements

In the 1950s my family emigrated to Australia and for a short time we lived in the Melbourne suburb of St. Kilda, one of many places given Hebridean names by earlier emigrants. Those names, heard for the first time on the other side of the world, acted like a magnet when I returned to Scotland, drawing me to all corners of the country including the Outer Hebrides. I have been back many times since and have again been able to enjoy the special atmosphere of islands (and the vagaries of travel) while compiling this book. A number of people assisted in that endeavour, some knowingly, others simply because they stopped to help, or willingly answered my questions. I thank you all. I must also thank the staff of the library, archives and museum in Stornoway, and Malcolm Macdonald of the Stornoway Historical Society for help in identifying the upper picture on page 85. The upper picture on page 80 was identified by Margaret MacKay and Chrissie-Anne Macarthur. I am grateful to them and to my fellow scribe Bill Innes who supplied the upper picture on page 28 and lower pictures on pages 29 and 36. Thanks must also go to Roslyn Anderson who let me use the lower picture on page 56.

Further Reading

Burnett, Ray, *Benbecula*, 1986.
Crofters Commission, *Guide to the Crofting Acts*, 1978.
Duckworth, C, and Langmuir, G, *West Highland Steamers*, 1967.
Gifford, John, *The Buildings of Scotland, Highlands and Islands*, 1992.
Haswell-Smith, Hamish, *The Scottish Islands*, 1996.
Hallewell, Richard, *Scotland's Sailing Fishermen*, 1991.
Herring Industry Board, *The Story of the Herring*, 1969.
Historic Scotland, *The Ancient Monuments of the Western Isles*, 1994.
Innes, Bill, *Old South Uist*, 2006.
Lo Bao, Phil, and Hutchison, Iain, *BEAline to the Islands*, 2002.

McCrorie, Ian, *Royal Road to the Isles*, 2001.
Miers, Mary, *The Western Seaboard, An Illustrated Architectural Guide*, 2008.
Ritchie, Graham, and Harman, Mary, *Exploring Scotland's Heritage, Argyll and the Western Isles*, 1985.
Scottish Vernacular Buildings Working Group, *Highland Vernacular Building*, 1989.
Steel, Tom, *The Life and Death of St. Kilda*, 1975.
Thompson, Francis, *Lewis and Harris*, 2009.
Thompson, Francis, *Uists and Barra*, 2009.

Introduction

In the not too distant past, mainlanders thought of the Outer Hebrides as remote. Yet, further back in time, when the sea was a highway and not a barrier, people made landfall on the islands. These early settlers left many reminders, especially the remarkable standing stones at Callanish. Other surviving remnants from prehistory include cairns, duns and brochs, and of these Dun Carloway is one of the finest. The defensive qualities of these structures will have been severely tested when a new wave of sea-borne settlers arrived from Norway.

The Vikings laid claim to the islands and left numerous place names as a reminder of their presence, although their most impressive legacy, the set of chess pieces found buried on the beach at Uig, on the west coast of Lewis, was almost certainly left unintentionally. After the defeat of the Norwegian King Hakon at Largs in 1263, the islands came under Scottish rule, but that was at best tenuous as local strongmen vied for superiority. Claiming the title Lords of the Isles, Clan Donald initially held sway, but powerful clans also established themselves locally: the MacNeills of Barra, a MacDonald branch, Clanranald, in the Uists and two branches of MacLeods in Harris and Lewis.

Hoping for support from the clans, Bonnie Prince Charlie landed on Eriskay in 1745 to launch his Jacobite Rebellion. He returned to the islands the following year as a fugitive, but escaped, leaving highlanders and islanders to face the government's anger.

Strictures were imposed, but the clan structure was still largely intact when the needs of the outside world began to intrude into island life. Industry on mainland Britain needed kelp, the product of burning the seaweed that clothed the islands' shores. Gathering and burning the seaweed was a labour-intensive activity, employing not just local people, but others who came to the islands to find work. Soon after the Napoleonic Wars the bonanza stopped and for many people that was the start of a perfect storm. Clan chiefs facing big debts began to sell their estates. The incoming landlords had no bond of loyalty either to their new tenants or the landless poor stranded by the collapse of kelp burning. Clearances began, with people moved off good land or forced to emigrate so that large sheep farms or sporting estates could be created. The islanders endured this treatment for fifty years, but in the 1880s new legislation gave crofters some hope. Protected by legal safeguards, land hungry people started to agitate for the farms to be broken up and, with the establishment of new crofts, the pattern of strung out communities became a feature of Hebridean landscapes.

Fishing and the weaving of tweeds grew alongside crofting as the mainstays of island life until the First World War, when many men were drawn into a fight far from home. Some died in action, others when the Admiralty yacht Iolaire foundered so tragically within sight of Stornoway. Those who did make it back wanted the 'homes (or crofts) fit for heroes' that the government had promised. A new landlord, Lord Leverhulme, had ideas to generate jobs through industrial development. In this clash of visions Lord Leverhulme chose to abandon his plans for Lewis and move to Harris. Emigration was again the only option for unemployed islanders.

The fragile island economies struggled through the Depression years and another World War. During that conflict an airfield was sited on Benbecula's grass airstrip and in the 1950s this facility was expanded into a military base for the most modern of warfare. After the 1960s, distances seemed to diminish as large car ferries were put on more direct routes and air travel became commonplace. Tourists came to admire the scenery rather than kill the wildlife, but the islands were also changing as crofting began to lose its appeal. With the dawn of a new millennium the harsh weather began to attract people trying to generate renewable energy. The elements that isolated the islands for so long, could yet become their greatest asset.

Fishing station at Castlebay in the 1930s.

Barra Head is the southern tip of Berneray, the most southerly of the string of islands that make up the Outer Hebrides. It is not, as the name implies, on Barra and, to compound the confusion, the lighthouse that takes its name isn't at the head, but is situated close to Skate Point, the most westerly point on the island. Designed by Robert Stevenson of the famous lighthouse-building Stevenson family, this sixty foot high tower was built with stone quarried on the island and lit for the first time in 1833. The island was deserted early in the 20th century, but the three keepers and their families remained as the only inhabitants until the light was automated in 1980.

Mingulay, Berneray's northern neighbour, was depopulated in 1912, so no islander will have known the Mingulay Boat Song, written in 1938 for the Glasgow Orpheus Choir. They will, however, have been familiar with the island's other claim to fame, the dramatic cliffs on its Atlantic coast. Sron an Duin, the one shown in this 1934 picture, is over 700 feet high and regarded as one of the highest sea cliffs in the British Isles.

The herring season was in full swing when this picture of Castlebay was taken around 1910. An upturned boat in the foreground is being used to dry nets while also apparently serving as the roof of a building. The adjacent buildings have more traditional thatched roofs. Sitting on its island in the bay, Kisimul Castle, the seat of Clan MacNeil, was the focus of the island's seafaring fame, a reputation underscored by the assertion that the MacNeil spurned a place on the Ark because he already had a boat. Celebrated in stories and song the Barra men's galleys were once dreaded by coastal communities as far away as Ireland, although fishing and farming had replaced raiding and reiving long before this picture was taken.

Seen here in 1936 the steamer *Lochearn* was not the prettiest boat on the water, but had comfortable first and third class passenger accommodation. She was launched at Ardrossan in 1930 and operated the mail route from Oban to the southern Hebridean islands. Her sister ship, *Lochmor*, launched a few weeks later, served the more northerly Hebridean islands.

Experts have long disagreed about the age of Kisimul Castle, but what is not in doubt is that it looks impressive, sitting on its rocky island. The seat of Clan MacNeil for over four hundred years, it was damaged by fire at the latter end of the 18th century and was still in a semi-ruinous state in 1838 when the MacNeil lands were sold by the then chief to pay off debts. The castle continued to deteriorate until 1937 when an American architect, Robert Lister MacNeil, who had been recognised as the 45th chief of the clan by the Lord Lyon, King of Arms, re-established the clan ownership. He began a restoration of the castle which was finished by 1970.

Streets built along straight lines are rare in Outer Hebridean villages, so the one facing the harbour at Castlebay is unusual. It is thought to have been largely built by masons from the north-east of Scotland whose work has created a distinctive location for the bankers, traders and restaurateurs who have set up in business there over the years.

Above & left: If Castlebay is viewed with the sea in the background, it is the castle that takes the eye, but the dominant feature of views that look inland is the church, as these pictures, taken on the beach in the mid 1930s, show.

Barra people are predominantly Roman Catholic and their main place of worship is the Church of Our Lady, Star of the Sea. It was built to the designs of Oban-based architect G. Woulfe Brenan and opened with a Midnight Mass on Christmas Eve in 1888. The picture was probably taken soon after that. A short time later the little thatched house, tucked in below the crag in the centre of the picture, was removed. A wall was built to enclose the church and an access drive created, but while many other changes have taken place around it, the church itself has remained a constant.

Above: Despite their boat handling skills, men from the islands tended to limit the scale of their fishing activities until well into the 19th century, mainly because they were a long way from mainland markets and local needs were small. Their capacity for preserving large quantities of fish was also limited, but despite this Barra men sailed for the Clyde every year with cured line-caught cod and ling. Some 30,000 fish were despatched in 1787 but with four out of five boats being lost making the trip a few years earlier it could be a hazardous way to earn some money. All that changed in the mid 19th century when full-time curers and fishermen from the north and east coasts of Scotland sought to make an early start to the herring season by moving to the outer islands in May and June. They set up a number of bases in the islands, but the principal ports were Stornoway and Castlebay where, as these pictures show, a large industry developed.

Right upper and lower: The British White Herring Act of 1860 required a registration number to be painted in white on a black background on each side of a fishing boat's bow. The number also had to be shown on sails and later on the funnels of steam vessels. Identifying letters were allocated to each port which then issued the numbers to the boats. The letters were usually the first and last of the port's name; these two boats come from Lowestoft and Yarmouth. That Castlebay had its own CY registration is an indication of its significance as a port.

The herring season peaked at different places depending on the time of year. People thought this was because the shoals moved from one area of sea to another, but with fish having slight variations - Barra caught fish tended to have more fat than others - it may be that different shoals inhabited their own parts of the sea and their patterns of movement were not as well understood as people thought. Such niceties were probably of little concern to these men who simply wanted to fill their nets and creels with saleable fish.

Fishermen preferred to deliver their catches to a market where, rather than having to sell at an agreed rate, competing buyers could push the prices up. The fish market, where these men have congregated, was therefore an important part of the herring trade. Tuesdays to Fridays were the busiest days with Saturday and Monday used to relax or repair damaged nets and equipment. Sunday was kept for religious observance, but with Barra a mainly Catholic island, the Protestant church was much busier than usual when the east coast fisherfolk were in port.

The fishing boats and men were not the only itinerant people associated with the industry; a large army of fisher lassies, like these, went from port to port wherever the fish were being landed. Some Barra women joined these gutters and packers in their travels.

After the fish had been landed and sold, they were tipped into large box-like troughs, known as farlans. The word is thought to have originated in Shetland where fish were formerly landed and cured at the 'foreland'. As the picture shows, the women stood beside the farlan, gutting the fish. It was cold, backbreaking, smelly work and the women often wrapped their fingers in rags to protect them from the sharp blade that they wielded at astonishing speed.

Another group of workers that followed the fishing fleets around were the coopers who made the thousands of barrels needed to pack the fish for despatch to their markets. The materials needed by these men - wood for the staves and iron for the hoops - had to be delivered by ships. These vessels also brought general supplies and became a familiar sight at Castlebay, especially at the start of the season when the curers set up their workshop and accommodation huts.

Before the First World War, the principal market for Barra-cured fish was Russia. Large ships would anchor in the bay and their cargoes of barrels, filled to the brim with cured herring, were ferried out to them in small boats that operated in a similar way to the barges or lighters that worked in large docks. After the war the Russian market was closed, so the emphasis shifted to other countries like Germany, the Baltic States and America.

The Protestant church, completed in 1893 to the designs of architects Hardy and Wight, is in the left background of this picture. In front is a funeral procession although it is not clear from the picture if the people have come from the church or somewhere else. In the 1930s, when the pictures on this page were taken, an island funeral would have followed tradition and such a procession would normally have left from the house of the deceased. The men formed up in two lines and walked in front of the six men carrying the coffin. It rested on a platform and was held aloft with poles that projected on either side. As the mourners proceeded to the graveyard the procession leader would direct three men from each line to step out and take over the duties of carrying the coffin when it passed. Women followed, and prayed. The grave was dug when the procession reached the cemetery and after the burial service, the grave was filled and the mourners dispersed.

Kentangval, to the west of Castlebay, was composed of the typically Hebridean thatched houses that early photographers liked to take pictures of. It was a crofting and fishing community, although the ability of men to take their boats out to sea was severely hampered by the narrow mouth of Loch Kentangval, an arm of Castle Bay. The loch's narrow entrance was confined not just by its banks, but also by a partially submerged rock that caused water to rush in and out. Known as 'the stream', this movement of water restricted boat movements and meant that villagers often had to leave their boats outside the bay. The village has changed somewhat since these early 20th century pictures were taken, with modern housing replacing all but a couple of the traditional buildings.

The islanders got a raw deal in 1840 when General Roderick MacNeil sold Barra to Colonel Gordon of Cluny for £38,000. He turned out to be amongst the worst of the clearance landlords turning people off the land and, when they languished in destitution, shipping them off the island. The colonel died in 1852, but the damage was done and his successor, Lady Gordon Cathcart, made little difference. The behaviour of landowners like the colonel came under the scrutiny of a Royal Commission, set up under Lord Napier in 1883. Its findings formed the basis of the Crofters Holdings (Scotland) Act of 1886, which coupled with subsequent Acts, turned the tide and gave crofters legal protection. This did not mean that crofting suddenly became an easy way of life, it was still subsistence farming, but some people were able to re-establish crofts on better land and there was security of tenure. The caption given to this picture when it was published as a postcard around 1905 was 'Crofters Stock-Taking in Barra'.

A different impression of crofting life is conveyed by this picture, which also shows an interesting latticework of ropes holding down the thatched roof. The building looks small and ill-kept, so may not have been used as a dwelling.

Above: The croft house in this picture was situated at Brevig, to the east of Castlebay. Ben Heaval rises prominently in the background. Houses like this are often referred to as 'blackhouses'. Possibly a misinterpretation of Gaelic, the term appears to have emerged in the late 19th century as a way of defining houses built without mortar and having a central fire with no chimney. Quite apart from looking very white, this little house defies such a description and has reached a high level of sophistication for a type of vernacular dwelling perfectly adapted to its environment.

It is not clear whether these women, dressed in their serviceable wrap around aprons, are carrying out the simple task of washing clothes, or if they are washing wool. Either way, an activity that required running water was not the simple task it is for people in modern houses with hot and cold water on tap, drainage and washing machines. The wringer mounted on the wooden tub is an interesting arrangement.

To a crofter the birth of a calf could mean the difference between being able to pay the rent or face a year of hardship, and so Barra's two cattle sales a year were vitally important. The one seen here was photographed in the 1930s.

The word kelp has two meanings, one as a type of seaweed, the other as the product left after seaweed is burned. Starting from around the middle of the 18th century islanders were encouraged to cut and gather seaweed, dry it and then burn it in shallow pits. Rich in alkali, the solid mass left behind was shipped to chemical manufacturers for use in a variety of products. The industry grew rapidly during the Napoleonic Wars when imports of the other principal source of alkali, Spanish barilla, were stopped, but when this trade resumed the demand for kelp collapsed leaving large numbers of people who had become dependent on the industry facing destitution and deportation. Kelp gathering continued on a small scale into the early 20th century, as this picture of kelpers' huts and carts on Barra shows.

Barra

In the 1930s, Barra's roads were not good. Rutted, pot holed and liable to puncture tyres and break springs, the state of the roads came to a head in 1937 when eleven of the twelve vehicle owners on the island refused to pay their road fund licenses. These unlikely rebels included traders, contractors, the doctor, two priests, two county councillors and the writers Compton Mackenzie and John Lorne Campbell. Summoned to the sheriff court in Lochmaddy, they admitted their guilt, but were all fined, charged costs and given the option of going to jail. Emboldened by largely supportive press coverage they appealed. The judge in Edinburgh criticised the sheriff, transferred the costs to the county council, quashed the threat of imprisonment and reduced the fines. The roads were improved the following year.

The cars in the foreground of this picture of the 1936 Barra Games represented about a quarter of the total number of vehicles on the island at the time. With Barra being the most westerly inhabited island in Britain, its games were easily the most westerly in the country too.

Held on the machair at Borve, the Barra Games was a highlight of the island year in 1936, and remained so in subsequent years. The great and good, appropriately clad in bonnet and plaid, put in an appearance and presented prizes. Here, sitting on a podium, deep in conversation, are Colonel Haldane, on the left, and Compton Mackenzie (later Sir Compton) who moved to the island in the early 1930s and lived there for some years.

Competition took place in the usual Highland Games events one of which, taking place out of picture to the right, appears to have attracted the attention of the crowd while the piping judges compare notes.

Barra

Here the judges gaze into the middle distance, listening intently, while the crowd just listens to the playing of a lone trouser-clad piper. In the foreground the girls seem distracted by other thoughts, perhaps rehearsing in their minds the dancing steps they are about to perform.

The unsophisticated, but evidently serviceable podium takes a pounding as the girls give their all in the dancing competition.

Not to be outdone by the young ones, the older ladies, the cailleachs, had their own dancing competition, giving substance to Mark Twain's assertion that: 'Age is an issue of mind over matter. If you don't mind it doesn't matter'.

When roads were rough and cars less reliable, a drive from Castlebay to Northbay involved a decision. The choice was between the shorter, hillier east coast route or the longer, flatter, better surfaced western route. At Northbay another decision faced the stressed-out motorist because, unusually for Barra, there was a road junction, with the road to Eoligarry and the north leading off from the circular route. This picture of the Old Inn contains another unusual feature - trees, something of a rarity on the islands, but which have taken root on Barra in greater numbers than elsewhere.

With its stone-built pier, Northbay was Barra's second harbour, a status that has been maintained with the more recent development of a much enlarged fishing quay and associated facilities. Northbay is a scattered community with at its core St. Barr's Church, just out of picture on the right. It was built in 1906 to designs by the same architect responsible for Our Lady, Star of the Sea at Castlebay.

GO BY AIR
BY NORTHERN & SCOTTISH

WITH Renfrew (Glasgow's Airport) as a base Northern & Scottish Airways cover a wide range of routes—to many of the leading centres in England, to Isle of Man, and Belfast. In the Highlands and Islands of Scotland, services are operated to Campbeltown, Islay, Skye, Barra and North and South Uist. On holiday, when time is so important, why not prove for yourself the undoubted economy and comfort offered. Write for a copy of full time-table and particulars.

NORTHERN & SCOTTISH
AIRWAYS LIMITED
HEAD OFFICE
AIRPORT FOR GLASGOW RENFREW, SCOTLAND

In the 1930s, when Captain David Barclay was looking for sites to land aircraft in the Hebrides, he met John Macpherson, also known as 'The Coddy'. He suggested the Traigh Mhor, a vast flat beach of sand bound into hardness by pulverised cockle shells. The captain liked the look of the beach and Northern and Scottish Airways began the island's first air service in 1936. The picture is from that year, but is thought to show a plane used as an air ambulance, a service that also made good use of the beach. Over the years the aircraft and operating companies changed, but services to Europe's only tidally dependent airstrip have continued into the 21st century.

Cockles have been gathered from the Traigh Mhor for as long as anyone can remember and at times have formed an important part of the islanders' diet. This little cockle gatherer from the 1930s was never likely to deplete the sands of shellfish, but more systematic cockling, to feed a lucrative export market, is thought to have contributed to the progressive wetting of the sands.

Bonnie Prince Charlie set foot in Scotland for the first time in July 1745 when he was put ashore on the beach at Eriskay, from the French ship *Du Teillay*. He spent the night on the island before moving on to gather support for his Jacobite Rebellion. At the time the island was owned by the MacNeil of Barra, and while he supported the Jacobite cause, he thought it better to let his tenants tend to their crofts rather than join the prince's army.

Father Allan McDonald, who had been parish priest at Daliburgh, South Uist since 1884, moved to Eriskay in 1893. His parishioners built a house for him, and then constructed St. Michael's Church using roughly dressed local stones. The timber came from ships' cargoes, lost or jettisoned and washed up on the shore. The maritime connections continued in later years with the addition of the bell from the German battle cruiser SMS *Derflinger* which had been scuttled at Scapa Flow in 1919. The bow of a lifeboat, washed overboard from HMS *Hermes,* was also later mounted below the altar.

The song, the Eriskay Love Lilt, has given the island an air of romance, but it is actually a rocky place, barely occupied until crofters moved there after being evicted from South Uist at the time of the potato famine in the 1840s. Faced with a choice of emigration or subsistence, they chose the latter and set about creating cultivable soil using organic material like seaweed and peat. This croft appears to be set on stony ground, with the house barely distinguishable from the rocks behind it, and there were plenty of stones to weigh down the thatch.

When these pictures were taken, the island's roads barely warranted the name, so the creels used as panniers across this boy's pony, would have been the most practical way of carrying heavy items. All this changed when the ferry to Barra and causeway to South Uist turned Eriskay into a vital link in the north/south road through the islands. The Eriskay pony came close to dying out in the 1970s, but with a concerted effort the survival of the breed was ensured.

To modern eyes it seems faintly incongruous to have a post office in a thatched cottage, but why not? These little buildings were the traditional vernacular structures of the area and the reality is that, when the post office on Eriskay was established in 1885, there would not have been any other kind of building for it to occupy.

Eriskay Post Office has evolved over the years from the little cottage in the upper picture, through the corrugated iron lean-to of the lower picture to the modern community shop. With telegraph communication installed well before the Second World War, the lines must have been buzzing in February 1941 when the Harrison Line freighter, *Politician*, went aground on Calvay Island in the Sound of Eriskay. Loaded with a general cargo that included a large quantity of whisky the incident inspired Compton Mackenzie's book and subsequent film Whisky Galore, although the movie deviated slightly from reality in that it was shot on Barra.

Having bought South Uist in 1838, Colonel Gordon of Cluny spent the next twenty years or so clearing people off the good land in the west. Some moved to the rocky east side of the island, settling at the head of Loch Boisdale. A tight, tricky loch to navigate, its east coast location was nevertheless an advantage in attracting steamers from the Scottish mainland, so it grew to become the island's principal port with all the trappings of a village. It is seen here about the 1940s or 50s looking west along the main road into the village, with the little mission church on the left and the bank and bank house in the centre of the picture.

This view of Lochboisdale, also from the 1940s or 50s, has been significantly changed by modern flats occupying much of the roadside leading to the pier. Behind is the distinctive Ben Kenneth, (Beinn Ruigh Choinnich) which becomes the focus of attention on the first Sunday of August when an annual hill race is staged. The route to the summit affords an opportunity for some competitors to shorten the run by swimming across the loch, although whether such heroics help or hinder is debatable. An elderly steamer sits alongside the pier, on the extreme right of the picture.

Lochboisdale

The steamer sitting behind a fishing boat in this picture of Lochboisdale Pier is the *Hebrides*, a general cargo and passenger boat built at Troon in 1898 for John McCallum & Co. They operated her between Glasgow and the Western Isles, calling at many places on the way and taking the best part of a week to make the journey. She also took passengers on trips to St. Kilda in the summer months. In 1929 John McCallum and a rival operator, the Orme Brothers, amalgamated to form McCallum, Orme & Co. and that company was itself absorbed by David MacBrayne in 1948. *Hebrides* remained in service with them until she was scrapped in 1955.

Boats like the *Hebrides*, sailing out of Glasgow, were superseded by ferries operating from more convenient ports and these in turn have given way to modern roll-on roll-off ferries. If this picture had been taken at any time since the installation of the access ramp for these ships, it would be filling the space at the end of the pier. Alongside are some fishing boats, a reminder that during the second half of the 19th century Lochboisdale also became a fishing port especially during the herring season when it was busy with boats, barrels and all the activity associated with the industry.

Many early travellers will have stayed at the Lochboisdale Hotel, built in 1882 to benefit from the trade brought by the building of a new pier. The hotel's main clientele were anglers drawn to the island to indulge their passion for trout fishing. It was badly damaged by a fire in September 1918 and remained disused for a number of years, but by 1936 it was promoting itself as 'the largest and one of the most comfortable and up-to-date in the islands'. The advertisement pointed out that there were 'seven mail boats per week during the season - two from Kyle, two from Mallaig and three from Oban' and this ease of access meant that a visitor could 'dine in London one night and Lochboisdale the next'.

The ruins of Calvay Castle sit on an islet off Calvay Island at the mouth of Loch Boisdale. It is old, but no-one knows when it was built or by whom. Like Kisimul Castle at Barra, it had an enclosure wall that followed the shape of its rocky base, while inside the wall were what are thought to have been a hall and a tower.

Situated at the cross roads to the west of Lochboisdale, Daliburgh is a sizeable township with facilities to match. One of these was its Higher Grade School, located in the corrugated iron building in the centre of the picture. It has since been superseded, but in its day had three classrooms where youngsters learned subjects as challenging as Latin and English literature. A fascinating account of schooling in South Uist is contained in the reminiscences of Frederick Rae who taught at the school at Garrynamonie, to the south of Daliburgh, in the late 19th and early 20th centuries. He was the first Englishman, and first Roman Catholic since the Reformation of 1560, to teach on the island.

The empty solitude of Loch Eynort conveyed by this picture from 1954 is not entirely natural. During the Clearances whole communities were forced out of this area to free up the best hill grazing on the island. To the north of Loch Eynort are South Uist's two highest mountains Beinn Mhor at 1994 feet and Hecla at 1988 feet. The loch also forms part of the boundary between the island's two parishes of Howmore to the north and Daliburgh.

The Outer Hebrides may possess one of Scotland's most iconic castles - Kisimul - but apart from it there were few such structures on the islands. Some buildings are called castles, but like Ormacleit Castle on South Uist, these were houses rather than defensive fortifications. A two storey, T-shaped mansion, Ormacleit was built in 1701 for Ailean, chief of Clanranald, but was burned down in 1715 and never rebuilt.

When the chiefs of Clanranald died they were buried a few miles to the north of Ormacleit at Howmore. Here a group of ecclesiastical buildings is clustered together in a manner redolent of early Irish religious sites, on ground that was once like an island surrounded by bogs. The ruins of two churches and two chapels remain while a third chapel was apparently demolished by the mid 19th century. The site may have been used in early Christian times although the oldest structure is thought to date from the 13th century, with the most recent, known as Clanranald's Chapel, built about 1574. The area still has religious significance because the Church of Scotland parish church was erected in 1858, about a hundred yards from the ancient chapels.

A post office was first opened at Howmore in 1843, as a sub-office of the main post town for the Uists, Lochmaddy. It became an independent sub-office in 1908 and a sub-office of Lochboisdale a couple of years later. Closed in 1951, Howmore Post Office was reinstated in 1965 although by that time it was located in more up-to-date premises.

Although partially obscured by a peat stack, this South Uist house appears to have been built with turf walls. Such buildings were not uncommon on the islands, being described in the 1880s as 'built of turf and thatched with straw or heather . . . the grass growing frequently on the tops of walls and roofs'. Inside there were 'some common boards put together for two or three beds . . . the fire was in the centre over which hung the pot . . . two or three large stones appeared to serve as seats'. The internal arrangements were therefore similar to those in stone houses, but poorer. The poverty of the people is evident although their baleful look might be a reflection of their attitude to rich photographers.

Grogarry Lodge dates from the time of the Clearances. Initially built as an early 19th century farmhouse, it was extended in the 1880s with the addition of the prominent central block when it became a shooting lodge. Situated close to Loch Druidibeg it is seen here with the mountainous east side of the island in the background.

Loch Skipport, one of a number of sea lochs that indent the mountainous east coast of South Uist, had a pier at the end of a four mile long road that gave the north of the island access to steamer services. The steep bends at the end of the road must have been hard going for ponies hauling loaded carts up from the pier to the more level track across the moors. The boat in this picture, the *Dunara Castle*, was built at Port Glasgow in 1875 for the Orme Brothers who operated her on regular services between Glasgow and the islands. Named after an ancient fortified site on Mull, she was a handsome ship and a good sea boat that became a familiar sight in the islands during her 73 years of service.

To the uninitiated, the most conspicuous creatures wandering freely on the Loch Druidibeg National Nature Reserve are ponies. Although delightful, these little animals are not the tough, hardy ponies that were once the work-horses of the islands. Stocky and standing at between thirteen and fourteen hands, the Highland pony is the largest of all breeds native to the British Isles. It was also formerly known as the Western Island pony, but interbreeding with stock from the mainland has diluted the pure island strain. It is also a very ancient type having been linked through fossilised remains to ponies that flourished before the Ice Age. The upper picture shows a pair of working ponies on South Uist. The other pictures show two good representatives of the breed: the pony in the middle was awarded first prize in the 1936 South Uist Show, while the lower animal, shown by a farmer from Benbecula, also won a prize at the show.

The east side of South Uist is rugged, mountainous and indented by rocky inlets, the west, fringed with glorious beaches, is a flat patchwork of machair, lochs and rivers. Roads weave though this wet landscape, clinging to the dry ground, but this option runs out at a number of places. One of these is Loch Bee, which the main north-south road crosses on a causeway, seen here in the 1930s. With an outfall on both east and west coasts, the huge, but shallow loch splits the island. Its fame used to be counted in the quantity and quality of trout that could be caught in its waters although it has come to be highly regarded by bird lovers for the number and variety of water birds that it hosts.

Those wonderful beaches on the west side of the island, facing the full rigours of the Atlantic, were (and still are) regularly clad in seaweed washed up by storms. It just lay there waiting to be gathered and burned for kelp by men like the one in this picture from about 1910. His hut, which will have been situated close to the shore, seems to grow out of the ground with a sunken floor, grass-grown earth walls and a roof clad with slabs of turf. The only concession to comfort in such huts was an east-facing doorway.

Fortified dwellings, or duns, and a bronze sword found in a peat bog are among the numerous archaeological remains that litter the area covered by the extended township of Iochdar, or Eochar. The little cottage, facing camera, has since this mid 20th century picture was taken, also become unoccupied and ruinous. The background however has been filled with the school, situated on the other side of the loch.

The two fords that gave Benbecula a tenuous low tide link to both South and North Uist were crossed around the turn of the 19th and 20th centuries, by South Uist schoolmaster, Frederick Rae. He described the South Ford as being a mile of wet sand with two deeper channels, both of which he jumped, after spurning the help of a local man who offered to carry him. When the tide turned, water rushing through these channels made the ford very dangerous, but an end to such hazards came a step closer in February 1939 when a favourable tide allowed the shallow draught coaster *Isleornsay* to ease into a specially marked channel in Benbecula Sound. She stopped long enough to deliver materials and machinery for the construction of South Ford Bridge. Completed in 1941, it was superseded by a full-width causeway in 1982.

There was an inn at Creagorry, on the Benbecula side of South Ford, for some time before the more famous hotel was built in the 1880s. Seen on the left of this picture from about 1960, it was erected by an Ayrshire builder who had come to the island to build schools following the passing of the 1872 Education Act. He also brought with him a working horse, a stallion, that is reputed to have greatly improved the blood line of island ponies. Creagorry also became the site of a store opened by the Scottish Co-operative Wholesale Society in June 1942, in effect coinciding with completion of South Ford Bridge. It was the 32nd retail store opened in what the SCWS regarded as 'Co-op deserts'.

Dun Borve, or Borve Castle, was a simple rectangular tower with very thick walls that has been in a ruinous state for longer than anyone can remember. Situated near Liniclate in the south-west corner of Benbecula, it is thought to have been built in the latter half of the 14th century by Lady Amie, the first wife of John of Islay, Lord of the Isles. After being divorced by him, she lived on the island estates that she had inherited from her brother, after his death. The lands were granted to Ranald, son of John of Islay, in the early 1370s although what use Clanranald made of the castle is not known. It is seen as a ruin in this early 20th century picture.

The North Ford looks delightfully tranquil in this picture, but the prospect of trying to cross it, however far out the tide, must have daunted many early travellers. Frederick Rae, who was shown the line of the ford by his friend Father McColl, described the path as being about four to five miles long, across 'mud and water interspersed with islets and black rocks'. It was 'forbidding', 'treacherous' and so narrow in places that a traveller straying a yard or two either side would rapidly be swallowed up by quick-sands.

The dangers of crossing the ford came to an end in September 1960 when a causeway, going by way of Grimsay, was opened by Queen Elizabeth, the Queen Mother. She arrived at Benbecula Airport from Dyce (Aberdeen) and sat down to lunch with selected civic and military dignitaries, while the band of the 4/5 Battalion Cameron Highlanders (T.A.) played outside - she always did like the sound of the pipes. Lunch over, the Queen Mother is seen here leaving the base in a police patrol car that had been specially brought over from Fort William. It took her to the southern end of the causeway where the opening ceremony was held and then carried on to Lochmaddy, before returning to Benbecula for the return flight to Dyce.

At Clachan the main road round North Uist meets the road to and from the North Ford. The latter is seen in the left foreground heading across the little bridge over the inlet to Oban a Chlachain, a lochan that reaches to within a few hundred yards of Loch Eport, a long finger of a sea loch that cuts across from the east coast almost creating another island. The direct road to Lochmaddy runs past the buildings on the right, one of which has long been the location of the local store.

Before the advent of car ferries, steamers like *Dunara Castle* and *Hebrides* called at many places that were either difficult to get into or had no pier, so they stood off while small boats ferried people and goods to the shore. On Loch Eport the *Hebrides* was met about halfway up the loch by this boat operated by the steamer's owners. With their heavy boat loaded somewhat haphazardly from the larger ship, the crew are seen here getting underway with one of them bending an oar and the others setting the sail.

Annual fairs and sports have long been a feature of North Uist life, as this picture entitled 'A Uist Market' shows. It was taken around 1900 and is a splendid depiction of the way people lived. Ponies are prominent, either as means of travel or to be bought and sold, and the stall on the left, an amalgam of trestle table and makeshift shelter, is not unlike the temporary stalls that people erect at present day markets.

Cattle shows and sales were important events on North Uist, as on the other islands. This sale took place at Clachan in 1936 and evidently attracted a sizeable crowd of men who are seen here casting an experienced, discerning eye over the animal in the pen.

First, second and third prizes were awarded at the North Uist Show for a wide variety of categories. These were not restricted to livestock, but included dairy produce, baking, yarn and home made woollen goods. Roddie MacDonald, who was a winner in the garden produce competition, is seen here proudly displaying his prize vegetables.

Situated at Claddach Kirkibost and originally built in the 1870s as a doctor's house and surgery, Westford Inn is the epitome of a 'four-square' building. The walls are almost as high as they are wide and the roof rises to an apex crowned with chimneys. The picture from the 1930s, however, only shows the front door with the then licensee, John MacAulay, outside.

Roman Catholics living in the islands to the south often faced persecution and eviction if they resisted attempts by landowners to force them to engage in Presbyterian worship. A similar situation arose on the west coast of North Uist, but here it was the form of Presbyterian worship that caused the trouble. At the centre of this was the crofting community of Paible, seen here scattered around Loch Sandary. The cause of the difficulties was The Disruption, the rift in 1843 that split the Established Church of Scotland in two and resulted in the formation of the Free Church. Parishioners who came out in favour of the Free Church built a shelter on common ground, but it was demolished by the factor who also evicted some of the more prominent dissenters and fined others.

Undaunted by the factor's tactics, people continued to worship in the open air and endured wind, rain and sleet in 1847 to listen to a visiting minister who preached from the doorway of a cow shed. Later, services were held on the knoll known as Creag Hasten, which was crowned by a large rock that gave the preacher some protection from the weather. Since these tribulations, Paible has grown into a substantial community.

Rows of pitch pine pews face the pulpit on three sides and paraffin lamps provide artificial light for the simple, unadorned interior of Kilmuir Parish Church, seen in this picture from the 1930s. Formerly North Uist Parish Church, the T-shaped structure with squat battlemented spire was built to the designs of architect Alexander Shairp in 1894. Situated beside the main road, it replaced an older church that sits as a ruin in the walled burial ground at nearby Hougharry.

There is scarcely any aspect of Hebridean land use that has not at some time been practised at Balranald. The MacDonalds made concerted efforts to drain and improve the land, but following the demise of the kelp industry cleared crofts to make way for sheep farming. Land raids in the 1920s re-established crofting, but about twenty years later some crofts were amalgamated to make a government demonstration farm. The austere Balranald House is seen here in the 1930s, about 100 years after it was built.

Scolpaig Tower, a 19th century folly, is octagonal in plan and two storeys high. It sits on a little island in Loch Scolpaig that was formerly occupied by an Iron Age fort and can be seen in the distance behind this artfully photographed post box on a post. Both the box and its post have been updated, the little croft house has become a ruin, but the folly remains intact!

The wide expanse of Vallay Strand separates the tidal island of Vallay from the rest of North Uist, but was it always so? Submerged peat deposits and tree stumps on the north of the island at the Bagh na Crobhag, and the extent of the strand itself, are seen as geological evidence that Vallay, and the whole of the Hebridean island chain, are slowly (very slowly) sinking, in contrast to the Scottish mainland which is very slowly rising. Vallay was inhabited from prehistoric times to the mid 20th century when it was abandoned. Vallay House, erected in 1902 for the island's then owner Erskine Beveridge, was itself left to the elements shortly after his son was drowned in 1944 attempting to cross the strand.

Loch nam Madadh was too good a harbour to ignore. It became the location of a cod and ling fishing industry in the 17th century and although that did not last, other activities followed. Boats carrying supplies and mails almost naturally headed for it and by the early 19th century the nucleus of the village of Lochmaddy had been established. It became a post town in 1843, confirming its status as the main settlement on the island.

Through the 19th century a clutch of civic or municipal buildings were erected at Lochmaddy. There was a court house, a bank, a school, another court house, a church and a poor house that became a hospital. The influx of trained professionals to work in these institutions contributed to the developing character of the village as it became the legal and administrative centre for all of the islands to the south of Lewis. The 19th century herring fishery and the growth of the ferry terminal all played their part too. In this picture from the 1890s, the bank is prominent on the left, with the old and new court houses on the right.

Originally built in 1827, the old court house was extended in 1845 and after being superseded in 1875 remained in use as a prison until 1891. It is seen here after 1900 when it became a depot of the Highland Home Industries Association which, as it says on the sign, was set up to market home spun tweeds. The sign also states that the Association's President was the Duchess of Sutherland - that's her standing outside with a bolt of cloth.

The new Sheriff Court house was built in 1875 to the designs of Inverness based architects, Matthews and Laurie. An extension was added in the 1890s.

The Caledonian Bank was based in Inverness and it used architects from the town, James Matthews and William Laurie, to design the Lochmaddy branch. The building was completed in 1877. A year later the bank, which had been in existence since 1838, was inadvertently caught up in the collapse of the City of Glasgow Bank and had to close for a few months. It reopened in August 1879 and continued in business into the 20th century, but never regained its former strength and was taken over by the Bank of Scotland in 1907.

Prior to the Education Act of 1872 a range of private and church schools, and accommodation for teachers, existed on the islands, although such provision was generally regarded as poor. To comply with the act, new schools, like the little one at Lochmaddy, with its larger schoolhouse, were built and all children between the ages of five and thirteen had to attend. This was never easy for widely scattered island communities and with public funds somewhat stretched, the children had to take a peat to school so that the room could be heated. No longer isolated on the edge of the village, Lochmaddy School has since been enlarged and the adjacent road significantly upgraded.

Lochmaddy Hotel has been extended on a number of occasions since the first part of the structure was built in 1863. A simple two storey building with three first floor windows, it can be seen sandwiched by the later developments in this picture from around 1900. In those early days its principal clientele were anglers attracted by the hotel's description of itself as a 'fishing hotel'.

Sponish House, the building behind this rickety looking footbridge, is a large and impressive mansion by island standards. Built for Lord MacDonald's factor at the start of the 19th century, it was used for some time as a lodge to accommodate those who had come to the island for 'sport' and became part of a seaweed processing business in 1956. That closed thirty years later, but subsequently a fire gutted the house leaving it in need of substantial restoration.

Loch Maddy is a maze of inlets and islets, bays and beaches, a superb harbour and an ideal location from which to conduct all sorts of marine activities. It has been known as a haunt of pirates, but also for fishing although never quite a herring port on the scale of Castlebay. There was a brief revival of the herring fishery in the 1920s, which perhaps accounts for the barrels stacked on the pier in this picture. The people are fishing for trout, an activity that the Uists are famed for. Indeed one notable guidebook of 1920 described North Uist as 'a shooting and fishing place' and that 'no one would go there with any other object than sport'. The tourist industry has changed its sales pitch since then!

Madadh, in Gaelic, means dog and Loch Maddy takes its name from two dog-like rocks of columnar basalt, Madadh Beag in the north and Madadh Mor to the south. They flank the entrance to the loch while a third rock, Madadh Gruamach, gloomy dog, sits further south. The 'maddies', as they are known, are seen in these 1930s pictures of the beacon on Weaver's Point that guides shipping in and out of the loch. The old beacon was replaced by an automatic light in 1980.

The Clearances affected every island in the Hebrides and each has its own story of cruelty. For North Uist the incident that stands out is that of Sollas, in the north of the island, where the women made a stand against those sent to evict them in 1849. Using stones as missiles and the hard stems of seaweed as sticks, they fought an unequal battle with the factor's men and police, but were eventually turned out of their houses. After a 'starving season' being moved around the island, some managed to find a place to resettle while others boarded an emigrant ship for a voyage to Australia that many did not survive. When the introduction of legislation brought redress, the crofts that were established were laid out as isolated holdings and not in the clachan, or village formation that had previously existed, so the landscape of scattered dwellings almost certainly differs from what would have developed in a normal evolutionary process.

Framed by a peat stack on the left and the house and outbuildings on the right, a woman on a North Uist croft is seen here feeding her chickens. The ladder laid along the wall head is an indicator of the constant need to keep the thatched roof wind and watertight.

Sheep may not have the most popular history in the islands, but their wool has long been the source of traditional crafts. With Ben Eval in the background, the foreground fence is festooned with fleeces, hung there to dry in the wind.

Amongst the many archaeological sites scattered across North Uist are a large number of Iron Age duns. Pronounced 'doon' the word is Gaelic for fort, which has an inappropriately militaristic sound to it, because these structures were primarily defensive. Many, like Dun Aonghais, seen here with Crogary Mor behind, were built on islands in lochs or other naturally defensible sites.

Dun Torcuill, in Loch an Duin to the east of Loch Portain, is also sited on an island. With thick galleried walls containing a cell and surrounding a 38 foot diameter courtyard, it is an impressive feature with characteristics similar to the tower-like structures known as brochs (see page 79). Access to these island duns was by way of a causeway like the one seen in the foreground. Built with boulders, they were not straight and would originally have been left just below the surface of the water to confuse anyone approaching with hostile intent.

Clach Mhor a Che is indeed a big stone (clach: stone, mhor: big), eight feet high, four feet wide and sixteen inches thick, standing on the west coast of the island looking across the tidal shore to Kirkibost Island. The heap of small stones on the left of the picture is thought to be the remains of a dun.

Poball Phinn is a stone circle, or more precisely an oval of irregularly shaped standing stones on partially terraced ground on the southern slopes of Ben Langass. Langass Lodge, which was built in 1870 as a shooting lodge and has since been converted into a hotel, can be seen in the distance, on the right. Beyond the lodge, on the northern slopes of the hill, is an 80 foot diameter chambered cairn known as Barpa Langass.

Although traditionally attached to Harris for administrative and ecclesiastical purposes, the island of Berneray in the Sound of Harris was physically joined to North Uist by a causeway in 1998. Thus linked it also became the terminal for the ferry to and from Harris, supplanting places on North Uist like Otternish that hitherto had been the location of inter-island ferries. In making the crossing to Harris, the modern boat has to weave between rocks and islands, and negotiate shallows, making this an unusually interesting ferry journey. This 1960s view of Berneray looks north across the bay known as Poll an Oir.

Before it became so well connected, Berneray was somewhat isolated and initially escaped the worst effects of the Clearances, but it was a well-tended fertile island and it attracted people evicted from Pabbay and Harris. This led to overcrowding and consequent evictions in the 1850s. One man who emigrated from Berneray was Angus MacAskill who at seven foot nine inches tall and thirty stones in weight was a giant. He died in Canada in 1863, but a memorial to him has been erected on his native island. Crofts were re-established early in the 20th century, when this picture was taken.

The story of St. Kilda is well-known. A self-reliant island community isolated by distance and wild weather, even from the island communities of the Outer Hebrides, 41 miles of storm-tossed sea from North Uist. For St. Kildans it was a happy idyll, free from the conflicts and tensions of the outside world and rarely bothered by anyone except the MacLeod of Harris' factor who came annually to claim the rent. It couldn't last. As the 19th century progressed a curious outside world developed the means to come and gawp at these natives on the edge of the world. People could also sit comfortably at home and gaze in wonder at images like this one captured by a photographer who will have come to the island on the steam ship lying in Village Bay.

Familiar with the savvy ways of the world, visitors often took advantage of the simple St. Kildans, but worse they brought infections against which the islanders had no immunity. They had no intellectual immunity either to combat the harsh brand of religion imposed on them by the Reverend John MacKay who was minister from 1866 to 1889. He demanded strict attendance at the kirk, full attention during sermons and rigorous observance of the Sabbath, with at times a detrimental effect on crops or animals. What produce the islanders were able to grow, and the sea birds like fulmars, gannets and puffins that they plucked from the dangerous island cliffs, were stored in the stone-built cleitean ranged above the village houses and seen in the foreground of these pictures.

The village, situated on the main island of Hirta, was laid out in the 1830s to replace the primitive early dwellings. Initially typical Hebridean 'blackhouses' were built end on to the 'street', each with its own plot of crofting land. The landlord had new houses erected in the 1860s by masons from Skye. They were stone-built, mortared, harled and had fireplaces and chimneys. The village also had a factor's house, church and manse.

In common with children all over the country, boys and girls on St. Kilda had to go to school. A schoolroom was attached to the kirk in 1898, but the number of children able to attend had been in steep decline for a long time owing to the prevalence of Tetanus Infantum, a disease that killed most of the babies born on the island. It is thought to have been caused by the treatment of the umbilicus with fulmar oil at the time of birth, although the bug may simply have lain in the container where the oil was kept.

Storms in the early months of 1912 prevented supply ships getting to St. Kilda and from early March to May people had to exist on tea, bread and butter. This perilous situation was discovered by the crew of a trawler who raised the alarm when they arrived in Aberdeen. The *Daily Mirror* newspaper quickly organised a supply vessel and the Admiralty sent HMS *Achilles* with emergency food supplies. Having raised the weather-imposed siege, the men of *Achilles* are seen here posing with some St. Kildans.

The St. Kildans also sold things to visitors and these men on HMS *Achilles* are seen painting birds' eggs obtained on their mercy mission in 1912. Buoyed up by their part in the rescue, the *Daily Mirror* newspaper started a campaign to establish a wireless transmitter, so that islanders could call for help if such a situation arose again. Arguments broke out over the cost of running such a facility and although one was set up in July 1913, it was dismantled the following April. Soon after that, the country was at war and a wireless station was built, to keep an eye on Atlantic shipping.

The wireless station drew attention to St. Kilda because a German submarine sailed into Village Bay in 1917, issued a warning to the villagers, and then fired some shells at the transmitter, damaging the church and store. There were no casualties, but this gun was installed to give the islanders some defence. It was never fired in anger. After the war, faced with diminishing self-reliance, exposure to disease and slow depopulation, the 36 remaining St. Kildans bowed to the inevitable and agreed to evacuate their island. They boarded the fisheries protection vessel HMS *Harebell* on 29th August 1930 and sailed to the mainland.

Through the 1930s the old steamers continued to take tourists to St. Kilda and some islanders, unable to settle on the mainland, took the opportunity of these cruises to visit their deserted village. The Second World War put an end to such adventures, but in the Cold War tension that followed, a missile-tracking radar station was set up on the island and this was later expanded into a larger military base. In 1957 the islands were bequeathed to the National Trust for Scotland, which organised voluntary work parties to protect the cottages. The island group was recognised as a World Heritage Site in 1986 for its wildlife and natural features, and this was extended in 2004 to cover the marine environment. A second award in 2005, made in recognition of the way people had existed in such a harsh environment for 2,000 years, made St. Kilda one of the few places in the world to have dual World Heritage status. Environmental groups also pay regular visits to study the wildlife, including the native Soay sheep. Some of these folk are seen in 2001 racing puffins in the Puff Inn, the island's pub (voted 'Pub of the Month' in 1974 by two Daily Mail journalists). So island life, of a sort, didn't cease in 1930 as had been expected.

In the late 18th century Captain Alexander Macleod of Harris erected warehouses and a mill at Rodel. He also promoted the development of the fishing and kelp industries, which helped to make the village into the island's principal port. Over time, as boats became larger they had to stand off the small harbour and with the rise of Tarbert as the main ferry terminal for Harris, Rodel slipped into quiet obscurity. The harbour, with Rodel Hotel on the left, is seen here in the 1970s with a fishing boat hauled up on what was once described as an 'excellent graving bank'.

St. Clement's Church at Rodel was built some time between 1520 and 1540 by Alasdair Macleod of Dunvegan and Harris, also known as Alasdair Crotach (or humpback). His tomb is one of two such monuments built into the structure; the other was for his son William. The building fell into disrepair after the Reformation and has since been restored a number of times, so that it remains as perhaps the finest church of its period in the Hebrides. Its most distinctive feature, the tall square tower (like a scaled down version of Scots vernacular tower house), was built on higher ground than the main structure. Access between the two is by way of a narrow stair within the walls.

At his large industrial works in Cheshire Lord Leverhulme made Sunlight Soap and it made him very rich. A restless, driven, determined man he acquired the Harris estate in 1919, but unlike the usual huntin', shootin' and fishin' Hebridean laird, he had ideas for industrial development. His main plan was to set up a large scale fishing and canning enterprise. He had been thwarted when he tried to implement a similar scheme at Stornoway, so turning his attention to Harris he transformed An t-Ob into a fishing port named Leverburgh.

Rocks were blasted on land to clear the way for a new road and at sea to ease navigation. A new pier was built along with sheds for fish processing and canning, a cooperage, a power house and housing for the workers. Briefly it worked, but did not have time to become an established industry before Lord Leverhulme's death in 1925. With his drive and financial backing gone, the venture was abandoned and the structures, seen here in the 1930s, fell into disrepair. It cost £250,000 to build, but a demolition contractor bought it all for £5,000. The place where all this activity took place has become the terminal for the ferry between Harris and North Uist.

When Leverburgh ceased to be a fish processing centre many of the people who worked there moved away, but village life carried on. These schoolboys, photographed in the 1930s with their head teacher, were learning gardening skills. Following the demise of Lord Leverhulme's venture the school took over the workers' recreation hall, Hulme Hall.

The Leverhulme Memorial School, as it is known, is on the left of this picture of Leverburgh. In front of the school is the Church of Scotland with the Free Church to the right of centre. Taken in 1939 from a vantage point on Bosival, the hill behind the village, the view looks across the Sound of Harris to the island of Pabbay (Priest's Island).

The more fertile machair lands of west Harris were cleared in the 19th century to make way for large sheep farms, but people began to return in the wake of crofting legislation. One re-established community was Northton where a new village, with houses on either side of the road like a mainland village, was created in 1902. The area abounds in impressive natural features like Traigh an Taoibh Thuath, a wide expanse of shell sand that, like the Traigh Mhor on Barra, was once used as an aircraft landing strip. The sands stretch from below Maodal, the hill on the right, to the Toe Head Peninsula and its distinctive twin-peaked hill Chaipaval, just out picture to the left.

Sitting on its own little headland below Chaipaval is this little ruined church, Teampull na h-Uidhe. With a view of Pabbay and a long tradition of religious uses, the site is thought to have also been occupied by a broch and an Iron Age fort before the 16th century church was built. It was superseded as the parish church in the early 18th century by the church at Scarista.

The shell sands continue up the west coast of Harris, a silver fringe to the machair lands where the township of Scarista Mhor is strung along the coast. It was created in the mid 1920s when the Department of Agriculture acquired estate ground and allocated it to crofting tenants. The process of erecting houses and establishing the crofts has been chronicled by a son of Scarista, writer and broadcaster Finlay J. MacDonald. The picture, taken from behind the Scarista Post Office, looks toward the island of Taransay.

When the name of Loch Langavat is rendered in modern English it reads as Lake Long Lake, the result of linguistic confusion between Gaelic and old Norse. This is compounded on the islands by there being at least five lochs called Langavat, three on Lewis, one on Benbecula and this one in south Harris. Situated in the hills to the east of Scarista and north of Rodel it is about two and half miles long and in places very deep. Abundant brown trout have drawn anglers to its peat-dark waters for many years as this hundred year old photograph shows.

A 1920s guidebook said of the road around the west side of South Harris that it 'cannot be called a cycling road' and listed the hazards: steep hills, stones, several gates and a winding route that required diversions over the grass. It has been much improved since then. The road is seen here early in the 20th century descending into Tarbert. In the centre of the picture, beyond the foreground buildings, is the Harris Hotel. Built in the 1860s, it can count amongst its guests the writer J. M. Barrie who scratched his initials on a dining room window. Had anyone else scrawled graffiti on the glass, they would have angered the management, but here the vandalised pane has been carefully preserved.

The building on the left of the upper picture is seen here as the premises of a 'Tweed Manufacturer'. Although he has not felt the need to call his product Harris Tweed, the cloth has spread the name of Harris across the world. The credit for this is of course due to a countless number of anonymous weavers, but also to the Countess of Dunmore who, following the purchase of Harris in 1834 by her husband, the Earl of Dunmore, became aware of the locally woven woollen cloth. She was apparently so impressed that she took it upon herself to promote it widely.

Making tweed starts, of course, with sheep, which have to be sheared to get the wool. For crofters, this was a communal activity as is seen here with some people, busily shearing their animals, having gathered them in a makeshift looking fank on a Lewis moorland.

This picture, used to promote Scottish Home Industries in Manchester in 1903, purports to show a woman in South Harris washing the wool after shearing.

Harris has pulled off a remarkable trick in getting the world to call the cloth after the island, because most of it was and still is made on Lewis. This picture, taken at Shawbost some time before the opening of the modern mill, shows people dyeing wool by boiling it over an open fire in a large cauldron-like vessel. The dyes were extracted from vegetable matter: yellows could be produced from willow leaves, bracken roots or groundsel; blue came from rib-wort; orange from ragweed, green from heather tips; even peat soot was used as a source for a cinnamon colour. A lichen known as crotal, scraped off the rocks, made a range of reds and if sorrel was added to the pot, the colours remained fixed for ever.

The image of granny at her spinning wheel was beloved by those who sought to promote a nostalgic vision of Hebridean life. Although this picture is staged, the activity was not, because women did have to spin the wool before it could be woven into cloth. That this was indeed women's work is illustrated by the man taking a sneaky look from the shed doorway in the top left hand corner of the picture.

Although many of the processes have been industrialised, for Harris Tweed to be genuine, and bear the famous orb trademark, it has to be hand woven in a crofter's home. Originally weavers worked on large wooden looms like the one shown here, but in the 1920s Lord Leverhulme introduced the iron-framed Hattersley looms to the islands. These were the mainstay of the industry until superseded by more modern machines.

When it came off the loom, tweed was loosely woven and had to be shrunk to make it firmer and washed to remove impurities like the grease and oil that were a sheep's natural weatherproofing. The best substance for achieving this was ammonia, and on remote islands the best source of such a chemical was human urine, which was carefully collected in a tub until required. This fulling process, known on the islands as 'waulking the cloth', also thickens the cloth by partially felting it. It has become a folk custom, but these Harris women were doing it for real. Working with a roll of material in the foreground of the picture, they are wetting it and pounding it to the rhythm of songs that helped maintain an even tempo.

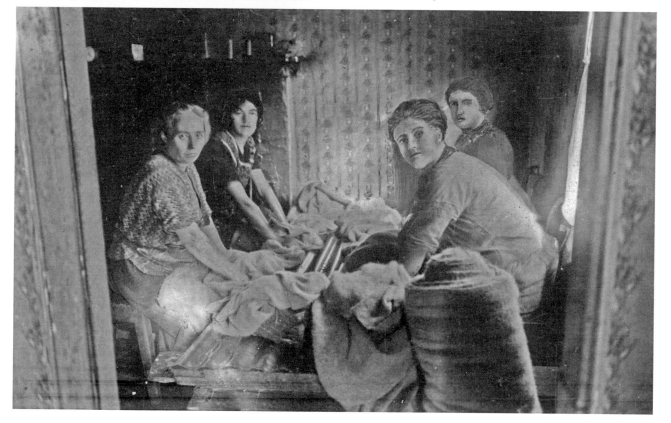

Tarbert

There are a lot of Tarberts in Scotland and although the spelling may vary slightly (Tarbet, Tarbat) the meaning of the name remains constant: an ithsmus. In historical times people used these narrow necks of land as places where they could haul, or even carry (portage), a boat between the bodies of water on either side. The narrow land bridge between North and South Harris is clearly evident in the background of this picture of Tarbert Pier, from around 1900. The steamer is thought to be David MacBrayne's *Lochiel*.

The ship seen here at Tarbert Pier in 1979 is the second in MacBrayne's fleet to bear the name *Hebrides*. Launched at Aberdeen in November 1963, she made her maiden voyage the following April and for the next 21 years plied the triangular route between Uig in Skye, Tarbert and Lochmaddy. She was fitted with a hoist in front of the bridge that allowed vehicles to be driven on board and lowered to the car deck. A cumbersome arrangement compared to modern roll-on roll-off ferries, it was at the time a huge advance that resulted in such a large increase in tourist traffic that the accommodation available on the islands was unable to meet the demand.

Scalpay Pier, seen in this Edwardian picture, was a lifeline for the island until 1997 when a bridge was built to connect it to the Harris mainland. With an economy that was, for a long time, based on a thriving fishing industry, the island, which sits at the entrance to East Loch Tarbert, has also played a key role in navigation. Eilean Glas, one of the first four lighthouses in Scotland, and the first in the Hebrides, was built on Scalpay in 1789 by the engineer, Thomas Smith.

It takes a brave and skilled boat handler to sail out into the Minch, to the Shiant Isles. Twelve miles due east of Scalpay these remote islands are made up of spectacular rock formations that have more in common geologically with Skye than Harris or Lewis. The writer Compton Mackenzie bought the islands in the 1920s and renovated an old cottage where he went to get peace and solitude, to concentrate on his writing. The picture, taken from Eilean an Tigh, shows the photographer's little boat in the Bay of Shiant with Garbh Eilean behind.

The high ground above the southern shore of East Loch Tarbert provided a favourite vantage point for people with a camera looking for a definitive view of Tarbert. With its pier, hotel, shops, tweed warehouses and street of whitewashed cottages, it was a substantial village that visitors were naturally attracted to. This picture and the view of West Tarbert on the facing page were almost certainly taken on the same day around 1900.

As the principal port for Harris, Tarbert has grown into a sizeable village with the main commercial development taking place around the ferry terminal and the roads leading to it. This view of the village shows it before the area in the foreground was laid out as a car park. Many buildings have been replaced, but some remain, most notably the 19th century corrugated iron Tarbert Stores, facing camera on the left. Just above it to the right, the two storey Bank of Scotland building is also still doing business.

The school, on the left of this view of West Tarbert, was built in 1896 and must have been quite new when the picture was taken. Since then the flat ground in front of the old school at the head of West Loch Tarbert has been reclaimed and much of it taken up with a hostel for children from outlying areas, a playing field and new school, as educational provision for Harris expanded over the years.

Since the school playing field was established on the foreshore, boys can play football where this lad once played beside a boat. For Hebridean children, growing up could be a magical time, with miles of shoreline to explore and heather clad hills to wander over. This boy, however, appears anxious to grow up as he measures himself against the boat, perhaps imagining the day when he will go fishing in such a craft.

The guidebook from 1920 that was critical of the road south from Tarbert, rated the one to the north as 'not bad' (high praise indeed!). It described the climb at Ardvourlie as 'terrific' and recommended that anyone 'driving' the 35 miles to Stornoway should wire ahead to Balallan for a fresh horse. The road is seen here as a narrow, winding track in a picture that probably predates the First World War, with West Loch Tarbert on the left and the school on the right. Since then, there has not only been significant development of the school and related facilities, but the road has been much improved, traffic has increased and demand for hired carriage horses at Balallan has slumped to zero.

To the uninitiated, the fact that Harris and Lewis are part of the same land mass and not two separate islands is confusing. As if to add to the confusion the border is not drawn at Tarbert, but between Lochs Resort and Seaforth, where the hills divide Harris from the flatter land of Lewis. The mountainous nature of North Harris is evident in this view of the old Ardashaig Bridge. The bridge has since been superseded by a much improved road, and modern houses sit beside the road to the west, which is seen here as a thin line going to the left, while the main road climbs round the base of Sgaoth Iosal.

In the early years of the 20th century the government encouraged Norwegian companies to establish whaling stations in Scotland's northern and western islands. One of these was set up by Captain Carl F. Herlofsen at Bunavoneadar on the south coast of West Loch Tarbert. The mess and smell were awful and fishermen thought that whaling would damage their industry, but it was given official support because it brought jobs to remote places.

Operating in the North Atlantic the whaling boats brought their catches to Bunavoneadar for processing. To do this the dead animals were drawn out of the water up a slipway, which is seen here with the crew of the whaling station. The trade was halted by the First World War, but started again after it. Lord Leverhulme bought out the Norwegian operators in 1922 and began processing whale meat, either for sale in Africa, or as cattle feed and fertiliser. As with Leverburgh the operation ceased after Lord Leverhulme's death.

The 7th Earl of Dunmore's hunting lodge, Fincastle, was built in 1867/68 beside a fine salmon river. The Scots baronial style used by the architect David Bryce was a bit incongruous for a Hebridean setting, but the mansion became a feature of the area and acquired a new name, Amhuinnsuidhe. Situated in such a remote location, the house was equipped to cope with any emergency, but when a fire broke out in the east wing annexe in 1936 the fire engine failed to work. Estate workers formed a bucket chain and did what they could to contain the blaze. The Stornoway fire brigade, with two drivers to share the strain of the 45 mile journey over rough roads, arrived to find that the fire was out. The solid old gable of the original building had contained the blaze.

This Land Rover fire engine, photographed at Tarbert in the 1970s, would have come in handy at Amhuinnsuidhe in 1936.

The road to the west used to carry on past Husinish to the jetty from where boats crossed to the island of Scarp. The island's last occupants left in 1971, so Husinish, with its little harbour and gently curving beach of glorious golden sand, effectively became the end of the road.

Situated at the head of Loch Erisort on the Stornoway to Harris road, Balallan is regarded as the longest village in Lewis. In this picture, the houses are more modern than traditional thatched cottages, but peat is still evidently in use.

Peat was traditionally the crofters' fuel. It was cut from banks where the decaying roots of mosses, heather and other plants had built up into a decaying mass that could be cut, dried and burned. The process started with the surface vegetation being lifted off the strip to be worked and placed out of the way where it would continue to grow. Having exposed the underlying peat a man with a bladed implement sliced slabs of peat from the bank, which were then laid to the side to dry.

Peat

The process of drying the cut peats began with them being turned regularly, depending on the weather. After two to three weeks the peats were placed on edge in little stacks so that air could circulate around them. When sufficiently dry they were taken off the moor. This was commonly done using a creel borne, not across the shoulders in the style of a modern rucksack, but with a rope or strap held tightly across the carrier's chest. This woman is carrying her well-loaded creel in this way, while her slightly stooped posture puts the weight on her lower back and buttocks. It was common for women to knit while carrying a creel so that their hands were never idle.

The woman in the upper picture is wearing leggings, but has taken to the moors in bare feet, as has the woman in this picture, cheerfully topping up her male companion's burden. His creel is also held across the chest and shoulders with a rope strap, although, sensible fellow, he is wearing boots.

In terrain with rough roads or no roads, peats were carried in creels strapped like panniers across the backs of ponies. The cailleach riding side saddle on her pony shows that these tough little animals could carry prodigious weights.

Creels were often used just to carry the dried peats to the roadside from where they would be taken away in bulk, in carts. This picture of boys with a peat cart was taken near Balallan in 1903. Tractors later replaced ponies in hauling the carts.

Great Bernera, the location of this crofter's house, ceased to be an island when a bridge was built to connect it to the Lewis mainland. Constructed in the immediate post-war era, when materials were in short supply, the engineers used a technique that required only a quarter of the steel normal for a reinforced concrete structure. This was sufficiently remarkable for a model of the 108 feet long bridge - the second longest of its kind to be built - to be exhibited at the 1951 Festival of Britain. The real thing was completed in 1953. Another key moment in Great Bernera's history, and in the crofters' struggle for legal protection, came in 1874 when men from the island and Uig marched to Stornoway to challenge Sir James Matheson over evictions. Three crofters were arrested and tried, but acquitted. The eviction notices were withdrawn and the estate factor lost his job.

Sir James Matheson, who bought Lewis in 1844, created a number of sporting estates on the island, one of which was centred on Loch Morsgail. Extending to over 13,000 acres of moors and hillsides largely devoid of trees it was, with no intended irony, known as a deer forest. The Victorian gentlemen, who came to hunt, shoot and fish wild creatures, stayed at the lodge which was erected on the loch shore in the 1870s and can be seen on the right of this picture.

The Royal Mail introduced the concept of the Postbus in the late 1960s. The idea that a postie, delivering mail in a sparsely populated rural area, could also provide a local travel service was a boon to scattered communities, although Hebridean postmen had unofficially been giving local people lifts in their vans for some time. This vehicle was photographed in 1979 outside the Timsgarry Post Office, the functions of which have since been relocated to the nearby Uig Community Shop.

RAF Aird Uig was a Cold War radar facility set up in the 1950s. The original equipment was superseded quite quickly, but the station, seen here in 1979, remained in use as a communications base until the year 2000. It was expected to close, but in 2003 NATO erected new masts to monitor activity across the North Atlantic. Some new uses have been found for old accommodation blocks.

This picture of Garynahine Hotel was taken in 1925, and used in the same year as a postcard. Nessie, who wrote the message on the back, is critical of the picture because, having described Garynahine as 'a lovely spot', she goes on to say that 'you don't get a real idea of it at all from this. It's much nicer'. Sadly her upbeat attempts to promote the area's potential for general tourism failed to stop the hotel becoming a shooting lodge soon after.

One of the most important archaeological sites in the country is the stone circle at Callanish. Dating from approximately 3,000 BC it had been almost entirely covered by peat by 1857 when Sir James Matheson had the surface deposits removed to discover the true scale of this remarkable site. What was revealed was not just the circle, but its attendant avenues and a small cairn that had been robbed in antiquity. The head of Loch Roag was clearly a place of some significance with up to twenty other prehistoric sites within a short distance of the Callanish circle.

Brochs appeared some time in the Iron Age and may have continued in use until about 200 AD. Unique to the north of Scotland, they may have evolved from earlier duns and are thought to have been defensive dwellings although who the enemy was or why the shape evolved here and nowhere else is a mystery. Dun Carloway is one of the finest surviving examples, to some extent because the way it has collapsed on one side has exposed the internal structure of the walls like a cutaway model. About fifty feet in diameter and over thirty feet high, it was perhaps only about ten feet taller when originally built.

The division of land into crofting strips is clearly evident in this view of Carloway from Ben Iomhair. Lord Leverhulme was drawn to Carloway because he wanted to develop it as a fishing port linked to Stornoway by rail. The plan failed, although some work was done to improve bridges on the Pentland Road, a direct route between Carloway and Stornoway that was begun in the 1890s, but never properly completed, despite a large amount of public money being spent on it over about twenty years.

Park House, Carloway, is thought to have evolved from a single storey structure used as a Free Church school and schoolhouse. Superseded by educational reforms, it became a private house in 1916 and the upper storey was added in two phases in the 1930s and 50s. In the 1950s, the owners, Donald and Christina Mackenzie provided teas, with scones and oat cakes, to the passengers of bus tours operated by MacBraynes. They also produced this picture postcard so that people could buy a souvenir of their visit.

Many things have been washed up on the west coast of Lewis, but few have been used to such dramatic effect as the whale that landed on the shore at Bragar in 1922. The huge animal had been harpooned out at sea, but got away from its pursuers before succumbing to the mortal blow. Its jawbone was set up in this arch with the harpoon that had killed it, suspended from the apex.

The straggling crofting township of Barvas sits at the junction of the west coast and Stornoway roads: this picture, probably taken about the 1920s, shows the road heading north to Port Nis. Barvas was thrust into the spotlight at the start of the 21st century when a proposal was made to establish a big windfarm on the moorland to the east and, although that idea was rejected, the attractions of the moor to energy producers remain.

Numerous burns and the Barvas River, the longest in Lewis, drain off the moorland into Loch Mor Barvas. The bridge in this picture, also probably from the 1920s, has been superseded by the modern road.

The Barvas Inn building is old by Hebridean standards, so it may have had a more spirited past before being run as a temperance establishment. It became a sporting lodge in the 1920s.

There is a huge contrast between Lews Castle and almost everything else on the island. Not only is it a large, imposing mansion, but the surrounding grounds have been landscaped and planted with a variety of trees. The castle was built for Sir James Matheson between 1847 and 1851. A native of Sutherland, Sir James, working in partnership with another Scot, William Jardine, made his fortune trading with China. Much of their early success was based on opium, but they also traded in tea, silks and other commodities, building the Jardine, Matheson business into one of the giants of colonial commerce. Having acquired Lewis, Sir James spent large sums of money on developments throughout the island and in Stornoway.

Lady Matheson is credited with planting much of the woodland surrounding Lews Castle, taking advantage of her husband's connections to import species from the Far East. The extensive conservatories, filled with exotic plants, will have helped the Mathesons to assuage any feelings of nostalgia for far away places.

The interiors of the castle were decorated with panelling and ornamental plaster work, and filled with fine furnishings that included paintings, tapestries and crystal chandeliers. These pictures show the ballroom (upper), drawing room (centre) and library (lower). Many of the interior features were removed by Lord Leverhulme when he bought Lewis from the Matheson family in 1918. He had grand plans for developing industry on the island, but ran into such concerted opposition that he sold out after five years. Before doing that he gifted Lews Castle and its grounds to the people of Stornoway.

In the 1970s, road improvements on the Scottish mainland allowed large roll-on, roll-off ferries to work between Ullapool and Stornoway. Before that, ships had operated between the island and the railheads at Kyle of Lochalsh and Mallaig, or the even longer route to and from and Glasgow. One of the vessels on that long run was *Clansman*, seen here at Stornoway in a picture taken some time before 1905. Launched at Govan in 1870, she was built to replace an earlier ship of the same name that ran aground on Sanda Island the previous year. The second *Clansman* operated without mishap on the Glasgow, Oban, Stornoway route until 1909 when she was withdrawn.

One of the ships that worked between Stornoway and the mainland was *Loch Seaforth*. Built in the Denny shipyard at Dumbarton, her construction was delayed by a lack of materials after the Second World War. She was launched in May 1947, but continued shortages affected her fitting out, so her maiden run to Stornoway did not take place until 6th December 1947. When it did, islanders were happy, because she could punch her way across the Minch half and hour faster than her predecessors, helped by the high bow and squat superstructure seen clearly in this picture of her leaving Stornoway.

The crowd on the Stornoway harbourside in this picture is thought to have gathered to mark the end of the First World War. The war had a profound effect on the island with a high percentage of those who served in the forces or merchant marine being killed or injured. After the war was over, the island's pain was compounded when, on 1st January 1919, HMY *Iolaire* foundered on the Beasts of Holm with the loss of 205 men. That they survived the war to die within sight of Stornoway Harbour must rank as one of history's most heart-wrenching tragedies. The names of those who lost their lives, both in the *Iolaire* disaster and in action, were commemorated on the impressive war memorial erected on a hill just outside the town and unveiled in 1924 by Lord Leverhulme.

A steamer's arrival was often eagerly anticipated in Stornoway, but the appearance of the Canadian Pacific liner *Metagama* outside the harbour in the 1920s was less welcome. She had called to pick up some 300 emigrants who were leaving Lewis to start a new life in Canada. It wasn't so much the ship that troubled people it was what she represented in the years after the First World War. She, and the other Canadian Pacific ships that followed her, were seen as taking away the island's future and consigning those who remained to uncertainty and decline. As if to underline the finality of the departure a man from North Tolsta had asked a friend to set fire to his house so that it could be seen burning like a beacon as the ship sailed for the new world.

Stornoway was known as a fishing port well before the herring boom began in the second half of the 19th century. Local men pursued cod, ling and other species, while northern Europeans and Dutchmen, working out of Stornoway, availed themselves of the rich pickings around the islands. These men were serving their own home markets which enjoyed herring long before the British developed a taste for the fish, but when they did, the number of boats working out of Stornoway in the season increased rapidly. This created a need for a more organised market which was met by the construction in 1897 of the distinctive octagonal building seen here. It was demolished in the 1970s, but a new steamer terminal that echoed the shape was built in 1998.

The market could be a busy place as this picture from about 1905 shows. The herring industry peaked at about this time and slowly declined in the years running up to the First World War. It lost some valuable markets during the war and never fully recovered afterwards, but the fishermen adapted and Stornoway has remained an important fishing port ever since.

One of Lord Leverhulme's schemes was to expand the Stornoway fishing fleet and develop processing industries to handle the anticipated catches, but his plans failed to win local support. On one level he was right, island fishermen were often at a disadvantage compared to their mainland counterparts. They did not usually have the money to buy their boats, so they borrowed from the curers, but rarely made enough to do anything other than repay their debts. Because of this they always tended to be equipped with last year's model so, by the time the islanders' fleet consisted of the finest sail fishing craft ever built, such as those in the foreground of this picture, the east coast boats were steam-driven. Steam boats were faster and more manoeuvrable and could always make port while a sailing vessel could be held back or stopped by a contrary wind. With a perishable cargo on board, this could be frustrating or financially damaging for men using such boats. Despite this, island fishermen were not averse to trying their luck as far away as East Anglia.

The scale of the herring fishery is clear from this picture of Stornoway with the forest of boat masts, gutters and curers at work and barrels stacked as high as the buildings in the background.

Stornoway developed in much the same way as many old Scots towns, with a principal thoroughfare (Point Street) leading to and from a castle. Originally a stronghold of Clan MacLeod, the castle sat on a promontory commanding the harbour approaches. It was confiscated in 1598 by King James VI, who handed it to settlers known as 'The Fife Adventurers'. Their attempts to 'civilise' the islands failed and when they left in 1610 the Mackenzies, the MacLeod's old adversaries, took over. Oliver Cromwell's troops arrived in 1653 and, having built their own fortification on Goat Island, cemented their authority by destroying the old castle the following year. The remaining ruin was finally obliterated in 1882 when the steamer pier was built on the site. As the castle's importance diminished, the beaches on either side of the promontory grew in significance and streets facing the harbour were developed. North Beach Street is seen here looking toward the steamer pier, in a picture from around 1900.

Perceval Square, which is seen on the right foreground of the upper picture, occupies the corner at the east end of North Beach Street. It is seen here in a picture from the 1950s, looking towards Cromwell Street with the Square Restaurant, where folk used to wait for their bus, on the left.

The mid 17th century Cromwellian occupation force was not universally popular, so the change of name from Dempster Street to Cromwell Street is a puzzle. Still, what's in a name? By any other the street would have become Stornoway's principal shopping thoroughfare. It is seen here about a hundred years ago looking west towards the building to the right of centre, that was erected in the late 19th century on the site of the former town house or tollbooth. Still referred to as the Town House, it was never actually used for the civic function implied by such a name, but has for many years served to house a Chinese restaurant.

Cromwell Street is seen here in 1954, about fifty years after the upper picture was taken. In common with high streets all over the country, large national stores like Hepworths soon disappeared. The name of the bank also changed in 1969 when the British Linen amalgamated with the Bank of Scotland.

An Lanntair Arts Centre has, since 2005, occupied the site in the right foreground of this picture looking east along South Beach Street. In the centre is the former Stornoway Town Hall, which was opened by Lord Roseberry in 1905. As well as the hall and the usual offices for the conduct of burgh business, the building contained the public library and reading room, one of many in Scotland to benefit from funds provided by the Scots/American industrialist Andrew Carnegie. The hall was being used as a YMCA institute during the First World War when, on 2nd March 1918, it caught fire. Some important books and documents were saved, but the library was destroyed and the building badly damaged.

The hall was reopened in 1929 by another transatlantic benefactor, T. B. MacAulay, president of Sun Life Assurance Company of Canada. He had provided funds for rebuilding, and restocking the library. Some external details of the building were altered, which helps to date this picture to some time after the reopening. Local government in the Western Isles was for a long time split with Inverness County Council running Harris, the Uists and Barra, and Ross and Cromarty responsible for Lewis. Calls to change this to a single authority for the islands grew after the Second World War, but had to wait until local government in Scotland was reorganised in 1975 and Comhairle nan Eilean Siar (Western Isles Council) was set up with a headquarters in Stornoway.

The Nicolson Institute's Secondary School in Francis Street is seen here in a picture taken within ten years of its building in 1896. Just short of 100 years later, having been superseded by the modern school, the building was adapted for use as Museum nan Eilean.

The Technical School in Stornoway was built by a local contractor Ross & Mackenzie to the designs of Edinburgh architect Hippolyte J. Blanc. He presented a souvenir gold key to Lady Pentland who is seen here, back to camera, performing the opening ceremony in August 1910. Lady Pentland was accompanying her husband, Lord Pentland, the Scottish Secretary, on an official visit to the Western Isles. Travelling on the fisheries cruiser *Minna*, they visited Barra, Vatersay, North Uist and Harris before arriving on Lewis where his lordship met with delegations of school boards, crofters and district nurses. Some of their itinerary was disrupted by bad weather, showing that the business of government could be tricky before the advent of air travel.

The Nicolson Institute is known throughout the country as a place of excellence in education, unless of course young people from Lewis are just brighter than average. The school, initially intended for the education of local boys, was founded with a bequest from Alexander Nicolson, a Stornoway born engineer who died in Shanghai in 1865. The original 1873 buildings are seen here in a picture taken about 1909.

Superseded over the years by more modern school buildings, the original Nicolson Institute was demolished in 1975. Stornoway folk were not happy to see it go, but the clock tower was kept and incorporated into the designs of a sports centre erected on the site. Seen here in 1979, the characterful stone structure helped to relieve the stark severity of the precast aggregate panels of the new. After a mere thirty years another sports centre was built nearby and the old one was demolished, leaving the school tower still standing.

Health care in Stornoway has been enhanced many times since the original twenty-bed Lewis Hospital was built. It is seen here in a picture taken soon after its opening in 1896 by Donald Matheson, nephew of Sir James. Funding for the furniture and fittings came from a Toronto based publisher who was the grandson of Hector Sinclair of Goathill Farm where the hospital was situated. With the hospital having been superseded by the modern Western Isles Hospital its old gates have been installed at the driveway of a house in Goathill Road.

Another Stornoway hospital was the sanatorium erected on the edge of town to combat the prevalence of tuberculosis on the island. Situated beside the main north/south road and known as the County Hospital, it is seen here in the 1970s. It has since been closed and the site used for a modern business park.

The High Church and manse were built on the corner of Matheson and Goathill Roads in 1910 for the United Free Church, which had been formed ten years earlier through the amalgamation of the Free and United Presbyterian Churches. The two churches owed their origins to divisions in the Established Church of Scotland and their formation led to yet another split. Although a large majority of the Free Church Assembly had voted for the union, some opponents, mainly from the Highlands and Islands, decided to continue as the Free Church. A legal dispute then arose as to which Free Church was the true one and who owned the property and assets, worth many millions of pounds. It went all the way to the House of Lords and to the horror of the majority, the judgement came down in favour of the Wee Frees, as the dissenters were known. The level of outrage that greeted the decision prompted parliament to intervene and enact legislation in 1905 to settle the dispute equitably. This enabled the United Free Church to build its High Church in Stornoway, while the old Free Church remained as a strong influence on the religious life of the islands.

Eglais na h-Aoidhe - St. Columba's Church - at Aignish, just east of the narrow ithsmus that connects the Eye Peninsula to the main island. The church is thought to have been built on the site of St. Catan's 6th or 7th century cell, although the existing, roofless structure dates from the 14th century or later. It was used as a burial place in the 15th and 16th centuries by the MacLeod's of Lewis. A memorial cairn has also been erected close to the old church at Aignish, in recognition of a protest in 1888 when landless people agitated for a farm to be broken up to provide more crofting land. As a result of the protest, thirteen men were arrested, tried and imprisoned.

This picture was apparently taken at Garrabost, to the east of Aignish on the Eye Peninsula, or Point as it is also known. It was used as a postcard with a caption 'Natives of Lewis', a description that presented the men as a curiosity rather than civilised people, although the boaters and braces do look a bit odd.

The Eye Peninsula ends at Tiumpan Head, the most easterly point in the Outer Hebrides. The lighthouse here, a 70 foot high tower, was built in 1900 to a standard design developed for the Northern Lighthouse Board by David Alan Stevenson. It was fully automated in 1985. The pier used to service and supply the light was just along the coast at Portnagiuran, or 'Portnag' as it is known locally. It is seen here, along with the lighthouse, in pictures from the 1970s.

Going north from Stornoway, the road up the east coast of the island, by way of Tong and Back, peters out at North Tolsta. Going south from Ness there is no road beyond Skigersta. The gap between the two was no more than ten miles when Lord Leverhulme set about building a new road to close it, but as with his other projects on Lewis he ran into difficulties and it was never completed. Some significant work was done, especially the construction of the reinforced concrete bridge over the gorge beyond the Traigh Mhor at North Tolsta. The unfinished road has since become popular with walkers, some of whom tramp the route for charity. Lord Leverhulme was evidently enthusiastic about the project, using this curiously unimpressive picture entitled 'Road Making in the Lews' on his Christmas card in 1921.

With the demise of Lord Leverhulme's east coast road, people travelling north from Stornoway have to go the long way round up the west coast by way of Barvas and Borve to Ness where these pictures were taken. The one of the children dates from the 1920s, that of the croft houses (above) from 1953.